FREAKY FISH

SEA HORSES

BY MELISSA RAÉ SHOFNER

Gareth Stevens
PUBLISHING

Please visit our website, www.garethstevens.com. For a free color catalog of all our high-quality books, call toll free 1-800-542-2595 or fax 1-877-542-2596.

Cataloging-in-Publication Data

Names: Shofner, Melissa Raé.
Title: Sea horses / Melissa Raé Shofner.
Description: New York : Gareth Stevens Publishing, 2018. | Series: Freaky fish | Includes index.
Identifiers: ISBN 9781538202685 (pbk.) | ISBN 9781538202623 (library bound) | ISBN 9781538202500 (6 pack)
Subjects: LCSH: Sea horses–Juvenile literature.
Classification: LCC QL638.S9 S56 2018 | DDC 597.6798–dc23

First Edition

Published in 2018 by
Gareth Stevens Publishing
111 East 14th Street, Suite 349
New York, NY 10003

Designer: Katelyn E. Reynolds
Editor: Joan Stoltman

Photo credits: Cover, p.1 Bill Kennedy/Shutterstock.com; cover, pp. 1–24 (background) Ensuper/Shutterstock.com; cover, pp. 1–24 (background) macro-vectors/Shutterstock.com; cover, pp. 1–24 (background) Kjpargeter/Shutterstock.com; cover, pp. 1–24 (fact box)nicemonkey/Shutterstock.com; p. 5 Ubonwan Poonpracha/Shutterstock.com; p. 7 LuismiX/Moment/Getty Images; p. 9 bluehand/Shutterstock.com; p. 11 ekler/Shutterstock.com; p. 13 Reinhard Dirscherl/WaterFrame/Getty Images; p. 14 Dorling Kindersley/Getty Images; p. 15 _548901005677/Moment/Getty Images; p. 17 sergemi/Shutterstock.com; p. 19 By Richard Whitcombe/Shutterstock.com; p. 20 Frolova_Elena/Shutterstock.com; p. 21 Kjeld Friis/Shutterstock.com.

Printed in the United States of America

CPSIA compliance information: Batch #CS17GS: For further information contact Gareth Stevens, New York, New York at 1-800-542-2595.

Contents

Horses in the Sea? 4
A Fish Like No Other 6
Slow Swimmers 8
Life in Warm Water 10
Hungry, Hungry Horses 12
Dad's Got the Pouch 14
Unsafe Waters 16
Which Sea Horse Is Which? 18
Sea Horses and People 20
Glossary 22
For More Information 23
Index 24

Words in the glossary appear in **bold** type the first time they are used in the text.

Horses in the Sea?

With fins on its head, a plate-covered body, and a long tail, the sea horse is a rather strange-looking sea creature. Believe it or not, it's a kind of fish!

Sea horses are small and slow, which means life underwater isn't always easy for them. Luckily, they have some truly freaky features to help them survive. There's so much about sea horses that scientists still don't know, but what they do know is pretty wacky!

FREAKY FACT!

Scientists think over 30 species, or kinds, of sea horses exist, but they don't really know.

The scientific name of this sea horse is *Hippocampus comes*. *Hippo* comes from the Greek word for "horse," and *kampos* is the Greek word for "sea monster"!

A Fish Like No Other

Sea horses have a wacky backbone! It has bony rings attached to it instead of ribs like other fish have. Those bony rings make up its body and all of its tail!

Sea horses have a prehensile tail, which means it's able to hold on to things. They'll often wrap their tail around objects like plants or coral to keep from drifting around. They might even use their tail to hold on to another sea horse!

FREAKY FACT!

Sea horses can move their eyes separately and look in two different directions at once! Often, they'll watch for danger with one eye while looking for food with the other. Weird!

Swimming is hard for sea horses. They use their tail to hold on to seaweed and other objects to stay in one place.

Slow Swimmers

Like other types of fish, sea horses have fins to help them swim. A fin on their back, called a dorsal fin, allows them to swim upright. Their dorsal fin moves quickly back and forth, pushing them forward. Small fins on either side of their head help sea horses turn.

Inside their body, sea horses have an air pocket called a swim bladder. They can change the amount of air inside their swim bladder to move up or down!

FREAKY FACT!

Sea horses are the slowest known swimmers in the entire ocean. One kind of sea horse moves less than 5 feet (1.5 m) an hour!

Sea horses range in size from just 0.6 inch (1.5 cm) up to around 13.8 inches (35.6 cm). Small or big, all sea horses look pretty much the same.

Life in Warm Water

Sea horses live along the coast in warm ocean waters less than 65 feet (20 m) deep. A few species live near the United Kingdom in the colder waters of the Atlantic Ocean. They can't live in freshwater, but some kinds can live in brackish water, a mixture of salt water and freshwater.

Sea horses are often found living in coral **reefs** or areas with sea grass. These places give them many things to hold on to and hide in.

FREAKY FACT!

Most sea horses live alone or in male and female pairs, but a few species live in groups. A group of sea horses is called a herd!

Sea horses can be found along coastlines throughout the world!

Hungry, Hungry Horses

Even though they're quite small, sea horses eat a lot! Why? Sea horses don't have a stomach! Food moves right through their body and doesn't give them much energy, so they have to eat all the time just to stay alive!

Sea horses eat small **shrimp**, tiny fish, and **plankton**. They use their long, tubelike snout to suck up any **prey** that swims by. One sea horse can eat up to 3,000 tiny shrimp in a single day!

FREAKY FACT!

To eat, sea horses float near their prey very slowly and then quickly move their snout to suck the food in. When they do this, the bones in their heads make a popping noise that some scientists call a "snick." Weird!

Sea horses don't have teeth, so they swallow their prey whole. Eek!

DAD'S GOT THE POUCH

When sea horses are ready to **mate,** the female places her eggs into a special pocket on the front of the male's body called a brood pouch. The eggs stay inside their father's brood pouch for several weeks and then **hatch.**

After they're born, baby sea horses are carried off by the water and must survive on their own. Few in each group live to be adults, so sea horses mate over and over again to ensure there's a next **generation.**

FREAKY FACT!

Most sea horses choose one mate to be with for their entire life. A female sea horse's territory may be 10 times larger than a male's.

Baby sea horses are called fry. Depending on the species, there may be as many as 1,600 babies at a time or only six!

Unsafe Waters

The sea horse has many predators and is an easy treat because it's so slow. Crabs, sharks, rays, some types of fish, and birds, including penguins, find sea horses to be a tasty snack.

The only way sea horses can avoid being eaten is to hide, or rather, to already be hidden by the time a predator comes around. Luckily, they're great at hiding! Also, their plates—which are part of the reason why they're slow swimmers—make them hard to eat!

FREAKY FACT!

Sea horses can't fight off predators, but they can fight each other for territory, food, or mates using their tails.

Sea horses can blend in with their surroundings using **camouflage**. Some species can change the color of their skin to blend in, while others already look very much like their **habitat**!

Which Seahorse Is Which?

When scientists first started studying sea horses, they had a hard time telling one sea horse from another! Then, they figured out that certain species of sea horse have different numbers of bony body rings. Now, they just count the rings to figure out the species!

Scientists have even discovered a way to tell individual sea horses apart. Many sea horses have a bony bump on top of their head called a coronet. No two coronets are the same!

FREAKY FACT!

Sea horses live for 1 to 5 years. The smaller the sea horse, the shorter its life!

The coronet of a sea horse is just like a **fingerprint**—each one is different!

Sea Horses and People

Each year, millions of sea horses are caught and used as food and **medicine** in China. People also regularly try to keep sea horses as pets, but they can't survive long when taken out of the wild!

Their homes are also in danger. When coral reefs are harmed by pollution, fishing, and **climate change,** the sea horse and many other freaky, beautiful sea creatures have no place to live, no food to eat, and too many predators.

Using special tools to breathe, see, and swim, you can visit sea horses in their home!

GLOSSARY

camouflage: colors or shapes in animals that allow them to blend in with their surroundings

climate change: long-term change in Earth's climate, caused partly by human activities such as burning oil and natural gas

fingerprint: the pattern of skin on a person's fingertip that allows an individual to be identified

generation: a group of people or animals born about the same time

habitat: the surroundings where an animal or plant naturally lives

hatch: to come out of an egg

mate: to come together to make babies

medicine: a drug that a doctor gives you to help fight an illness

plankton: tiny plants and animals that float freely in water

prey: an animal that is hunted by another animal for food

reef: a long line of rocks or coral or a high area of sand near the surface of the water in the ocean

shrimp: a small shellfish that has a long body and legs and that is eaten as food

snout: an animal's long nose

FOR MORE INFORMATION

BOOKS

Curtis, Jennifer Keats. *Seahorses.* New York, NY: Henry Holt and Company, 2012.

Hansen, Grace. *Seahorses.* Edina, MN: ABDO Kids, 2015.

Turner, Pamela S. *Project Seahorse.* Boston, MA: HMH Books for Young Readers, 2010.

WEBSITES

Seahorse
kids.nationalgeographic.com/animals/seahorse/#sea-horse-grasses.jpg
View pictures of sea horses and learn more about these amazing creatures.

Seahorse Facts
theseahorsetrust.org/seahorse-facts.aspx
This site is packed with fun facts about sea horses!

Seahorses
dkfindout.com/us/animals-and-nature/fish/seahorses/
Visit this interactive website to learn more about sea horses!

Publisher's note to educators and parents: Our editors have carefully reviewed these websites to ensure that they are suitable for students. Many websites change frequently, however, and we cannot guarantee that a site's future contents will continue to meet our high standards of quality and educational value. Be advised that students should be closely supervised whenever they access the Internet.

INDEX

Atlantic Ocean 10
backbone 6, 18
brackish water 10
brood pouch 14
camouflage 17
China 20
climate change 20
coastline 10, 11
color 17
coral reef 10, 20
coronet 18, 19
eggs 14
eyes 6
fins 4, 8
food 6, 12, 16, 20
fry 15
herd 10
life-span 18
mates 14, 16
pairs 10
pets 20
plates 4, 16
predators 16, 20
prey 12, 13
size 9
snout 12
species 4, 10, 15, 17, 18
stomach 12
swim bladder 8
swimming 7, 8, 16
tail 4, 6, 7, 16
territory 14, 16